Auto Focus
CORVETTE

Auto Focus

CORVETTE

Richard A. Lentinello

FRIEDMAN/FAIRFAX
PUBLISHERS

A FRIEDMAN/FAIRFAX BOOK
Please visit our website: www.metrobooks.com

Library of Congress Cataloging-in-Publication Data available upon request.

ISBN 1-58663-157-8

Editor: Ann Kirby
Art Director: Jeff Batzli
Designer: Kevin Ullrich
Photo Editor: Jennifer Bove
Production Manager: Karen Matsu Greenberg

Front and back cover photography: ©Ron Kimball

Color separations by Colourscan Overseas Co. Pte Ltd.
Printed in China by Leefung-Asco Printers Ltd.

1 3 5 7 9 10 8 6 4 2

Distributed by Sterling Publishing Company, Inc.
387 Park Avenue South
New York, NY 10016
Distributed in Canada by Sterling Publishing
Canadian Manda Group
One Atlantic Avenue, Suite 105
Toronto, Ontario, Canada M6K 3E7
Distributed in Australia by
Capricorn Link (Australia) Pty Ltd.
P.O. Box 6651
Baulkham Hills, Business Centre, NSW 2153, Australia

Contents

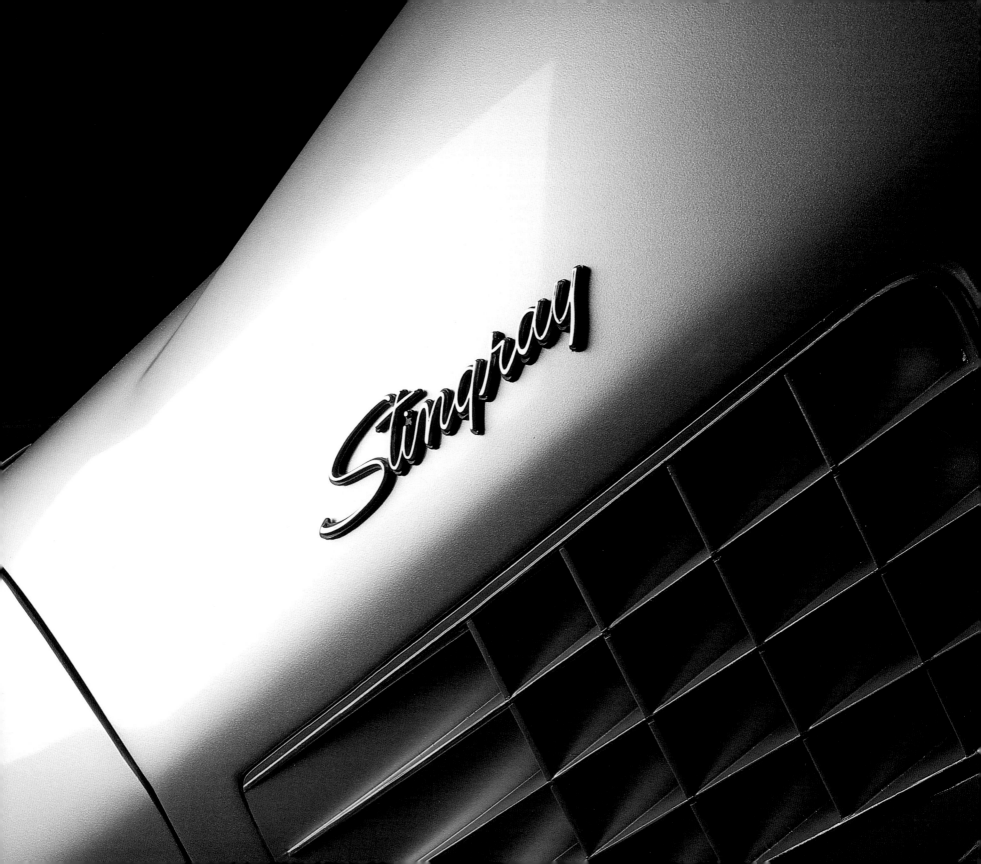

Introduction
The Corvette Experience

The sexy, wind-cheating fiberglass body and the powerful, earthshaking V8 that it hides are just two of the countless reasons why millions of car enthusiasts across the world are obsessed with the Chevrolet Corvette. The Corvette is a feast for the senses: its racy silhouette and cozy interior combine with fierce acceleration and road-hugging handling to create a unique and exciting driving sensation punctuated by the staccato rhythm of the engine's potent rumble. To touch it, sit in it, or drive it is to become hooked for life. In simple terms, the Corvette is an icon—America's symbol of road supremacy.

Ever since the Corvette's debut at General Motors' 1953 Motorama, held in New York City's posh Waldorf-Astoria Hotel, car enthusiasts have been crowding Chevrolet showrooms across America to sneak a closer look. Through the years the shape of the Corvette has evolved from a fifties-era cruiser complete with subtle tail fins to the graceful aerodynamic form of the contemporary high-tech C5. In between we welcomed the awe-inspiring Sting Rays of the mid-sixties, the sleek contours of the second-generation Stingrays of the 1968–82 era, and the streamlined fourth-generation models built from 1984 to 1996. While each of the five generations is distinctly different from the next, a family resemblance of artful styling cues ties them all together, maintaining that special Corvette look that is so prevalent in each and every model that Chevrolet has produced. The long front hood, the front fender side vents, the fastback rear, the four individual round taillights—these are the hallmarks of the Corvette style.

Adding to the mystique of these beautiful, powerful sports cars is the fact that they are a relatively rare sight on the road. With an average annual production total of only about twenty-five thousand cars since its inception, the Corvette's numbers are fairly limited in comparison to other domestic cars. The car is already a

Over the years, the crossed-flags emblem has adorned everything from the Vette's gas cap (above) to its steering wheel (opposite).

standout amid your average road fare; its rarity makes it all the more captivating. A speeding Corvette—driving past, hugging the ground with its engine growling—commands attention, respect, and even awe from everyone it leaves in its wake.

As if to laugh at the laws of economics, the Corvette has remained remarkably affordable despite its relative scarcity. From its potent V8 engine—which develops huge amounts of horsepower, torque, and neck-snapping acceleration—to its stable, gluelike cornering ability, the Corvette has consistently delivered the high performance of an exotic European sports car for the price of a fine domestic one. Perhaps this is the secret behind Corvette's status as the most successful sports car ever made.

As compelling as a Corvette is on the highway, it is on the racetrack that it really thrives. Corvettes have claimed victory after their hard-fought battles at speed on thousands of occasions. From the high-banking of Daytona to the twisting road courses like Riverside, Sebring, and Watkins Glen to the ultimate endurance test of man and machine at the 24 Hours of Le Mans in France, Corvettes have chalked up numerous class wins and overall victories through the years on both the professional and amateur levels of motorsports competition. And in quarter-mile (402m) action, Corvettes have literally ruled the drag strips of

America since the fifties with their massive amounts of tire-shredding horsepower and asphalt-melting torque providing blindingly quick acceleration.

The Corvette has enjoyed a long life span of competition success, due in no small part to its amazing tough-build quality and nearly bulletproof engines. Although there have been many engines of various displacements and horsepower ratings available through the years (including a straight-six from 1953 to 1955), both Corvette's small-block and big-block engines are engineered with some of the finest yet simplest design features, which help them maintain long-term durability regardless of how much their owners abuse them. Some of these special engine features include a five-bolt cylinder head pattern surrounding each cylinder to ensure maximum sealing of combustion gases and to minimize cylinder head warpage, meaty internal oil and water passages to prevent overheating, and an ideal ratio between bore and stroke dimensions and crankshaft journal width for optimal performance. If ever there was a "perfect" engine, the Chevrolet small-block is it.

Some of the other specially designed mechanical components that have remained unique to the Corvette include a fully independent rear suspension that is sprung via a transverse mounted leaf spring. In 1981, this leaf spring was replaced with a single fiberglass reinforced monoleaf spring, a design so effective it is used on the 1999 Corvette's front suspension as well as in the rear.

Yet the construction feature that has from the beginning set the Corvette apart from all other automobiles is its unique fiberglass body. The use of fiberglass was completely revolutionary in 1953, but its light weight and the fact that it would remain com-

pletely rust-free quickly garnered fans. The Corvette's shell is also safer in an accident than steel, as fiberglass can absorb far more of the force of an impact than steel can. Despite some difficulties involved in working with the material during the early years of production, the fiberglass shell quickly became the hallmark of the Vette, and has been a much-loved feature of every model built since.

This combination of a rust-free body, a simple engine design, and basic mechanical underpinnings has endeared the Corvette to the hands-on do-it-yourself crowd, the tinkerers and tuners who thrive on bringing their sports cars up to new levels of performance. Corvette maintenance is a straightforward exercise that many owners find very satisfying.

Of course, the early models have special appeal. Disassembling an old Corvette down to its bare chassis and rebuilding the entire car with new components, fresh paint, and a new interior can be extremely rewarding, and restoration of older Vettes is a hobby that borders on obsession. An entire industry has been built around supplying aftermarket parts to Corvette owners with everything needed to rebuild the perfect

beast: new body panels, engine and suspension components, chrome trim, wheels, and even upholstery kits.

Corvette ownership is like an addiction. Many enthusiasts, after sampling firsthand the thrill of owning the most fashionable automotive statement ever created, find themselves wanting to drive, tinker with, and, yes, own more than one. With five different generations of Corvette models to date—each providing its own unique level of driving characteristics—many fans crave at least one of each model so that they can savor the taste of the Corvette experience as it developed through the years. Other enthusiasts are drawn toward only specific models from a particular generation. Still others desire only convertibles or cars with big-block engines. The focus of a Corvette collection can be as diverse as the cars themselves.

Like many addictions, the Corvette is an indulgence that is savored in groups. With several hundred Corvette clubs scattered throughout the United States, Canada, and Europe, Vette fans don't need to go far to find a fellow aficionado. Shows, rallies, races, and even weekend cruises bring Vette lovers together; through newsletters and websites, members share tips on maintenance, preservation, restoration, and repairs.

The Corvette isn't just a car. It is a cornerstone of automotive innovation, an instantly recognizable icon of fun, freedom, and muscle on the American road. The reasons behind its success are simple and straightforward, yet at the same time complex and undefinable. There are the style, the speed, and the power, and then there is something more. The photographs in this book attempt to capture the subtle nuances and timeless aesthetic that have made the Corvette not just another fast and fun car, but an obsession, a first and lifelong love. Hop in, and enjoy the ride.

1953-1955
The First Corvettes

W hen the Corvette was introduced in 1953, it was billed as "the American sports car of the future." Indeed, its futuristic design contributed in some degree to its somewhat disappointing debut. The fiberglass body proved difficult to build for workers on General Motors assembly lines who were entirely unfamiliar with the material. Each body was assembled from many different pieces, all of which had to be glued together to form a complete shell. As workers struggled, production slowed, and only three hundred units were built that year.

Yet those first three hundred Vettes had an indelible impact on the American automotive market. As the first American entry into the European-dominated sports car market, the Corvette sparked the country's interest in racing-inspired two-seater roadsters. And while the '53 Vettes may have been underpowered and somewhat crude in terms of comfort and options, they set the stage for the future of American sports car design. And, as the rarest Corvette model, these then-unpopular cars are among the most sought-after by modern Vette enthusiasts.

All 1953 Corvettes were painted in Polo White with contrasting red upholstery and a black canvas convertible top. There was only one engine available— a 235-cubic-inch straight-six called the Blue Flame. With its three single-barrel side-draft Carter carbure-

The 1955 roadster (opposite) was the first Corvette powered by the famous Chevrolet small-block V8 engine. The driver's side door mirror on the '53 model (above) is a prime example of elegant, simplified design.

tors it developed 150 horsepower; attached to it was a Powerglide two-speed automatic transmission. Performance was hardly spectacular compared to today's standards—or even in comparison with the European cars that inspired it—but without a direct competitor, American consumers were none the wiser. All the public knew was that the Corvette offered top-down driving excitement unlike anything they had ever seen before. But the key problem proved to be that the new Corvette was far out of reach for the average buyer, priced for only the wealthiest of wallets, and this poor marketing strategy haunted Chevrolet in later years.

The base price was $3,498. Add the only two available options—a heater at $91.40 and a signal-seeking AM radio for $145.15—and the cost jumped to $3,734.55, more than a luxurious Cadillac. This was a staggering price in 1953 and was, in truth, even more inflated considering that most of the mechanical, electrical, and suspension components were the same ones used in existing Chevy sedans that sold for less than half the price.

To eliminate the labor-intensive method of constructing the Corvette body, Chevrolet shifted production from its makeshift garage in Flint, Michigan, to a fully equipped modern factory in St. Louis, Missouri, in 1954. With production now more efficient, Chevrolet had the capability to build 10,000 Corvettes.

Yet only 3,640 were made in its sophomore year, and 1,100 of those remained unsold. The market that Chevrolet thought was big wasn't, and many potential buyers were still turned off by Chevrolet's elitist attitude from the year before.

To entice buyers, four colors were now offered: the original Polo White, Pennant Blue, Sportsman Red, and Black. All had beige canvas convertible tops, red wheels, and red interiors except for the Pennant Blue cars, which received a beige interior. Using the same mechanicals as the '53s, the '54s were slightly more powerful, producing 155hp.

With so many '54 models still unsold, production for the 1955 was reduced to seven hundred cars, thus making the '55 the second-rarest Corvette ever made. Although the exterior remained the same, a 265-cubic-inch V8 engine was made available as an option. With its 195 hp, the Corvette finally had the right stuff to go along with its sporty looks. And for the first time, befitting its sports car character, a three-speed manual gearbox was available. The '55 color lineup included Polo White, Pennant Blue, Corvette Copper, Gypsy Red, and Harvest Gold.

If it wasn't for Ford's introduction of the new 1955 Thunderbird, Chevrolet most probably would have killed the Corvette. But now they had competition to stand up to.

14

Pages 12–13: The first Corvette: the 1953 roadster. All three hundred examples built featured white lacquer exteriors with red vinyl interiors, red steel wheels, and black canvas convertible tops.

Left: The steering wheel's crossed-flags emblem reminded drivers of the Vette's sporting intentions.

The Blue Flame Special straight six (below) was the only engine available in the 1953–54 Corvette. Three single-barrel, Carter side-draft carburetors helped it develop 150 horsepower.

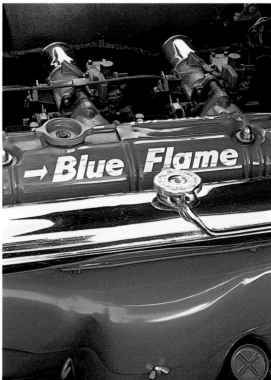

Startling for its era, the styling of
the 1953 Corvette featured a low,
aerodynamic profile with
minimum front-end overhang
and a trendy pair of winglets on
its shapely rear fender.

1956-1957
Classic Beauties

If ever there were to be an award for the prettiest car ever, Corvette enthusiasts would undoubtedly elect the 1956–57 by a unanimous vote. With its near perfect shape and balanced proportions, the design of this two-year-only body style is a simple one that doesn't rely on an overabundance of garish chrome trim to enhance its look. It's a masterpiece of transportation, with a dainty appeal that's uncommonly attractive for an automobile.

The 1956 model was the Corvette's first major body redesign since its introduction. Most of the deficiencies and build problems that plagued earlier models were eliminated, such as windowless doors and leaky tops. And with three years of experience in perfecting the use of fiberglass, the quality and practicality of construction were now far more acceptable. Doors with wind-up windows, exterior door handles with locks for security, and uncovered headlights for better lighting were welcome additions. The only noteworthy design element remaining from the 1953–55 models was the dashboard. This new body style also introduced side coves, allowing buyers to embellish their Corvettes with a two-tone paint scheme, while an optional hardtop made winter driving more tolerable.

The mechanicals were basically the same as before, with minor improvements made to the chassis. A new axle with an optional 3.27 ratio was fitted in the rear, while a 12-volt electrical system became

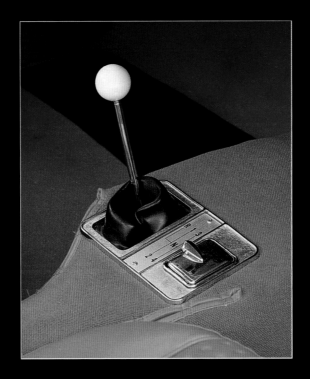

The prettiest shape to ever clothe a Corvette lasted for only two years, beginning with this Aztec Gold 1956 model (opposite). As seen on this 1957 fuelie (above), the racy white ball stick shift was a dainty, yet strong design.

standard. Performance also received a major boost due to a dual-quad carburetor option complete with dual-point ignition that pushed the 265-cubic-inch V8's horsepower to 225. Then there was the special-order Duntov cam—designed by chief engineer Zora Arkus Duntov, the godfather of the Corvette—that increased power to a startling 240 hp. But even the Vettes' base engines put out a respectable 210 hp.

The 1957 model was an identical twin only on the outside. Under the hood resided a larger 283-cubic-inch V8 with 220 hp. Power options were plentiful, giving buyers a choice of either 245 or 270 hp with dual-quad carbs or 250 or 283 hp with mechanical fuel injection, a Corvette first. Other first-time offerings included a four-speed gearbox; close ratio three-speed, heavy-duty racing suspension; and three extra rear gear ratios—3.70, 4.11, and 4.56.

A new palette of colors, including Polo White, Onyx Black, Venetian Red, Cascade Green, Aztec Copper, and Arctic Blue, added to the appeal of the 1956–57 models. Inca Silver was introduced on the '57 cars.

Finally, the Corvette was a legitimate sports car contender, with devastating performance and satisfying handling to match its good looks. In 1956, production rose to 3,467 cars; in 1957, it jumped to 6,339. The Corvette had finally arrived—it was the success that Chevrolet had dreamed it would be, and its future in the Chevy lineup was secure.

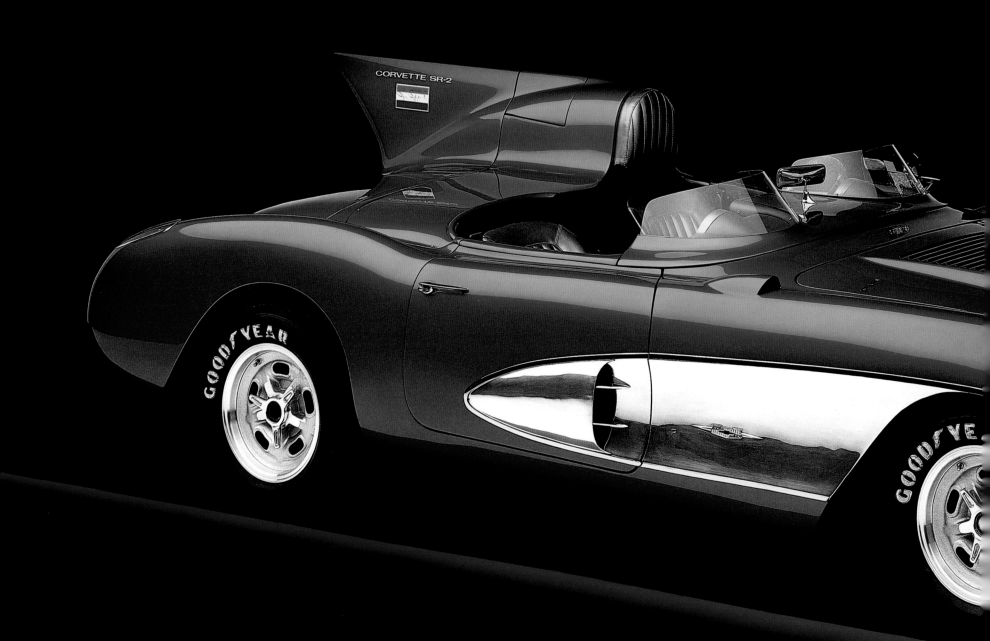

Based on a 1956 production model, the 1956 SR-2 (left) is one of the most celebrated Corvette sports racers ever constructed. A strong wood steering wheel (below) enhanced the driver's control with its better grip. A column-mounted tach was necessary to keep the engine in one piece.

Pages 22–23: The king of the solid-axle Corvettes: the fuel injected 1957 convertible, one of only 1,040 built.

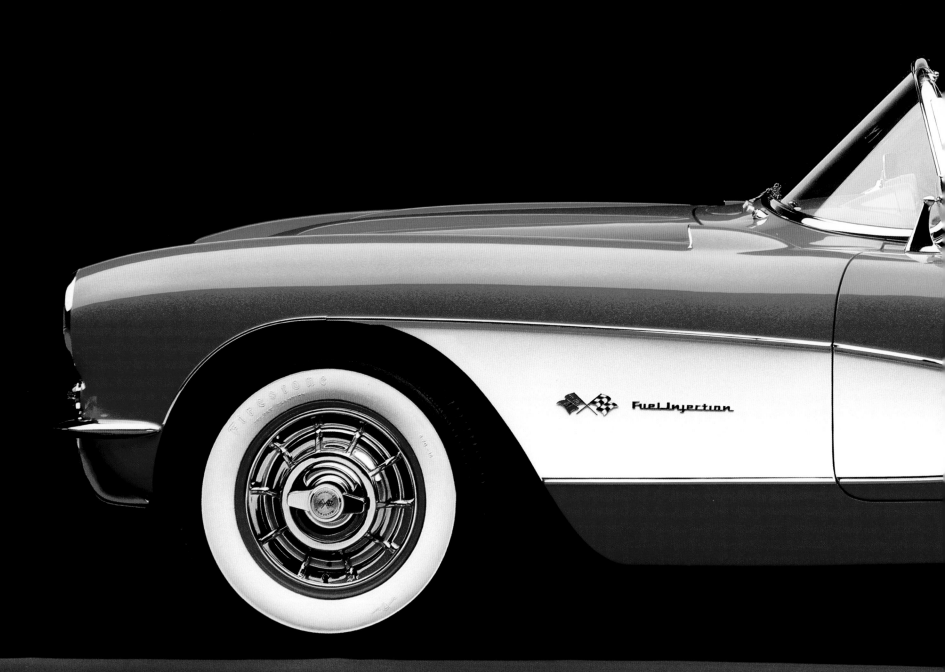

White painted coves and
whitewall tires (left) complement
the Aztec Copper color exterior,
supporting the fifties styling theme
with a natural period look.
Manufactured by AC, the column-
mounted tach body (above) was
painted to match the steering
column and dashboard.

Truly distinctive, this 1957
solid-axle Corvette (above)
features poverty hubcaps over
red-painted wheels, which match
the hardtop, and a fuel injected
283-cubic-inch V8 under the hood.
Unadorned for the times,
the rear styling on the '57 (right)
was very simple, yet very
attractive. The trunk was wide
but shallow.

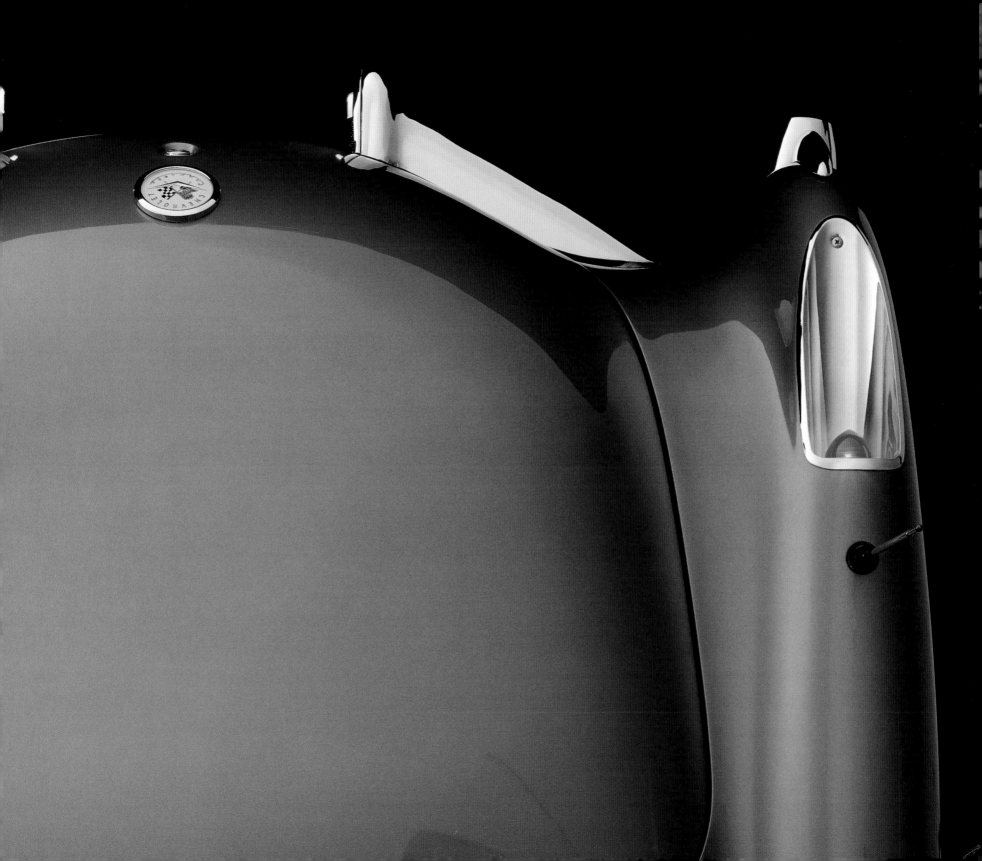

The year 1958 ushered in the era of automotive excess, a trend that the Corvette did not escape—the industry's taste for lavish chrome trim and decorative adornments influenced the '58 Corvette body style in a big way. Compared with the elegant design of 1956–57, the new Corvette looked positively muscular, disguised with frivolous design treatments like no other Corvette ever conceived. With its fake louvered hood and gaudy chrome spears on the trunk lid, the '58 remains a unique model.

But beneath the superficial embellishment was a Corvette that was superior to its older siblings. Its new body was wider, longer, and stronger, giving it a tighter, more solid feel. The most prominent exterior feature was the quad headlights, which lasted until 1962. On the inside, a new dashboard repositioned the instruments in front of the driver, a passenger-side grab bar was introduced, and a new center console and loop pile carpeting added to the comfort level.

Under the hood, the base 283-cubic-inch V8 now had 230 hp, with the top-of-the-line engine being the 290-hp fuelie. Those versions with quad carbs remained the same as the 1957, with 245 and 270 hp. The low-horse fuelie had 250 hp, but to complement the power, Chevrolet added a Heavy Duty Brake and Suspension package that included special shocks and springs, a thicker front antiroll bar, quick ratio steering, and finned brake drums

Restyled to keep pace with the excess-chrome trend of the late fifties, the 1958 models (opposite) featured a larger grille with separate chrome openings below quad headlights, a fake louvered hood (above), and a trunk lid embellished with a pair of chrome spears.

with metallic linings and individual cooling ducts. These components transformed the Corvette into a real road burner. Chevy built 9,168 of them by the end of 1958.

In 1959, the Corvette returned to its roots with a clean design that eliminated the louvered hood and the tacky chrome trim from the trunk lid. But beyond these cosmetic changes, the '59 was nearly identical to the previous year's model. Even the five engine options had the same horsepower ratings. Interior differences were small; they included thicker padding on the passenger grab bar, the addition of a storage bin below, and reshaped lenses on the dashboard gauges to reflect less light. For the first time, a black interior was available. Reaction was positive to the limited revisions: 9,670 cars were sold.

The idea of leaving well enough alone continued through the 1960 model year, and the public approved. With sales finally into five figures, with 10,261 cars sold, the Corvette finally reached—and surpassed—the 10,000 mark, the production goal Chevrolet had set six years earlier.

Identical to the '59 model both mechanically and aesthetically, the 1960 cars were the last Corvettes to incorporate the taillights into the rear fender tops and the exhaust tips into the bumper. It was also the last year of the imposing chrome grille with its large vertical bars. A more modern look was on the horizon.

In response to mounting criticism, the 1959 Corvette (below, left) featured cleaner styling, devoid of the '58's louvers and trunk spears, but the fake knock-off spinner (below, right) remained on the all chrome hubcap. Radical-looking louvers (right) vented engine heat on this one-off 1958 competition model.

30

Bolder and more muscular-looking than the 1956–57 models, the quad-light, three-grille front end styling (opposite) remained until 1962. This 1960 model is finished in Roman Red.

Corvette engines quickly became famous for their power, durability, and small size—hence their use by many European constructors to power their limited-production sports racers. This black beauty is a British-built Lister, powered by a 327-cubic-inch Corvette V8 fitted in a tube frame below a hand-formed aluminum body.

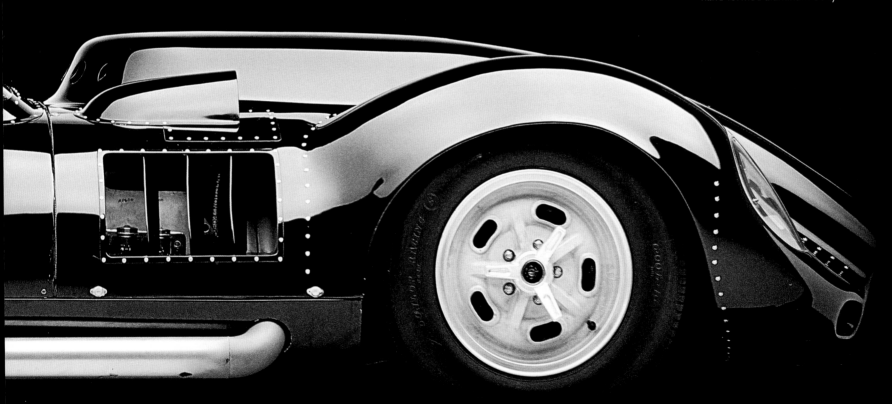

34

Much to the disdain of Corvette
collectors today, during the late
fifties and sixties many Corvettes
were customized, as illustrated by
this wild-looking '58 (above).
Note the large triple-earned
knock-off wheel spinners, hood
scoop, reworked grille opening,
and rear tail fins.

Unmistakably solid-axle Corvette
styling, the body shape on this
1960 Roman Red beauty (right) is
emphasized by the white painted
coves and wide white wall tires.
The tachometer was incorporated
into the dashboard for a more
integrated appearance (opposite).

1961-1962
Solid-Axle Screamers

The old saying "The more things change the more they stay the same" couldn't be truer when describing the 1961 and 1962 Corvettes. From the door handle forward, the cars looked identical to the 1958–60 models, yet the rear-end style was brand new. Actually, the reshaped tail was a hint of what was to come regarding the all-new Corvette still two years away. The '60 was an interim car, perhaps, but what an excellent car it was.

With the body style entering its fourth year of production, all the tweaks made through the years resulted in the best-built Corvette of the old era. The solid construction and fine build quality make it a real treat to own today—if you can find an owner willing to part with one.

In the mechanical department, all was the same. The chassis and suspension were carryovers, lasting until the end of the 1962 model run. Engine types were unchanged for 1961; however, there was a sound boost in the power department for the two fuelies. The base fuel injection engine went from 250 to 275 hp, while the high-horse fuelie went from 290 to 315 hp. The base 283-cubic-inch engine and the two midlevel versions with dual-quad carbs had the same horsepower as before—230, 245, and 270 hp, respectively.

The options list was much the same as the 1958–60 models. Two key options—the Heavy Duty

The 1962 model (opposite) differed only slightly from the '61 cars. The main exterior difference was the absence of the chrome trim surrounding the cove. "Design with a purpose" best describes the stick shift (above) on this 1961 model with blue interior.

Brakes and Suspension and the 24-gallon (91L) fuel tank—garnered little enthusiasm from buyers. As a result, Vettes stocked with these features are so rare that they are the two most sought-after options for collectors of classic Vettes today. If you find an old Corvette today fitted with either of these two rare components, don't hesitate for a moment—buy it!

In 1962 the fastest solid-axle Corvette of them all was introduced; this may have been the last year of the first-generation Corvette, but at least it was going out with a bang. The cause for such attention was the new 327-cubic-inch V8, an engine produced until 1968. Unlike the smaller 283, the new 327 was far more powerful, developed more torque, and revved easier and smoother. It transformed the old solid-axle cars into real screamers.

With the dual-quad carb option dropped, a single Carter four-barrel was the rule. Depending on its size, horsepower varied. The choice was 240, 250, or 300 hp, while the sole fuel injected version had a whopping 360 hp! Public approval was overwhelming, with 14,531 cars produced in 1962, compared to just 10,939 cars a year before.

The era of the so-called solid-axle or straight-axle cars is now over. As captivating as they were, the styling of these delightful roadsters is now held in high regard—they are true American classics.

One of the most attractive color combinations ever used on a Corvette: Ermine White with Sateen Silver painted coves (below).

38

Today, the 1961–62 Corvettes are increasingly sought after due to their distinctive blend of the original solid-axle styling with the newer Sting Ray rear. This customized yellow example (above) has later Chevrolet Rally wheels.

Right: The interior of the 1961 Corvette was virtually unchanged from the previous that of the previous generation. The last of the solid-axle Vettes, the 61–62 models are considered the best built Corvettes of the old era.

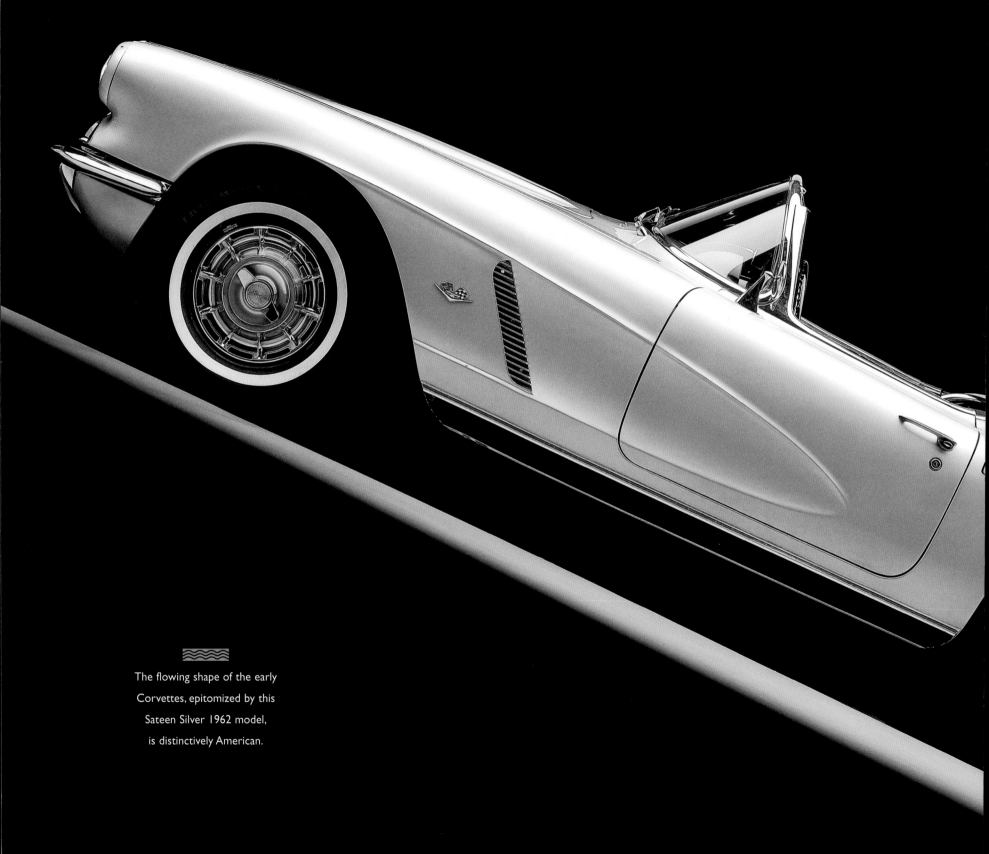

The flowing shape of the early
Corvettes, epitomized by this
Sateen Silver 1962 model,
is distinctively American.

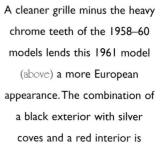

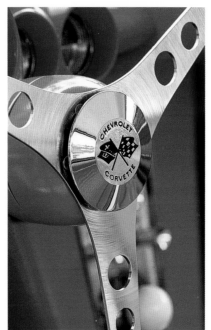

A cleaner grille minus the heavy
chrome teeth of the 1958–60
models lends this 1961 model
(above) a more European
appearance. The combination of
a black exterior with silver
coves and a red interior is
a Corvette classic.
Left: The crossed flags showed up
once again on the wheel of the
1961 Corvette.

Chapter Five

1963–1967
Midyear Madness

Corvette production went through the roof in 1963, with a total of 21,513 built. The Vette that broke the glass ceiling was the sensational new Sting Ray, a ground-up redesign so sleek and futuristic that it sent shock waves throughout the entire automotive industry, captivating the public's imagination like no other car before.

This was the first all-new Corvette since its inception ten years before, and the first with hidden headlights. It was built in two body styles: a coupe and a convertible, neither of which had a separate trunk. From its new exterior shape and modern interior design to its complete chassis and suspension system, the 1963 Corvette sported a design that evolved from a special racing car called the Mitchell Sting Ray. This race car was created by a group of Chevrolet engineers and designers, led by GM chief stylist Bill Mitchell, unbeknownst to General Motors' top brass. This unique machine received positive reactions wherever it was raced or even just displayed. Its crushing popularity made it a perfect inspiration for the next Corvette, and the new model was based on this proven design.

Under that lovely Sting Ray body was an all-new chassis that was far more rigid. The suspension was also new, introducing for the first time a fully independent rear. Its novel approach incorporated a transverse leaf spring that enhanced its handling, providing its occupants with a comfortable ride.

Three of the most sought-after Corvette coupes of all time: the 1963, 1964, and 1967 midyears (opposite, front to back), the first generation of Corvettes to be labeled Sting Rays. For one-off racing models, the original crossed-flag emblem (above) was used in conjunction with a second emblem such as this set used on the Gulf Oil 1963 Z06 coupe.

The engine offerings were exactly the same as those in 1962: the base 327-cubic-inch V8 put out 250, 300, and 340 hp, while the fuelie pumped out 360 hp. Three long-awaited options were leather upholstery, air conditioning, and true knock-off wheels made of cast aluminum.

Aside from its 375-hp fuelie V8, the '64 remained much the same. Visually, the major difference in the new coupe was the removal of the body split separating the rear window to increase rearward visibility. Thus the term "split window" refers to the 1963 coupe only. All told, 22,229 '64s were made.

Apart from restyled front fender vents, the exterior of the 1965 Corvette was unchanged, but four-wheel disc brakes and a big-block engine were finally offered. This special 425-hp 396-cubic-inch V8 was a one-year-only option, which paved the way for the even larger 427-cubic-inch monster the following year. The 1965 model was also the last of the mechanical fuel injected engines. With five different engine combinations, production increased to 23,562.

The 1966 Corvette had the largest production run of all the midyear models, with an amazing total of 27,720. Although it looked the same as the '65 version, the '66 Corvette sported two small-block and two big-block horsepower combos to make everyone happy.

The final midyear model was the 1967, the cleanest of them all due to its limited chrome trim and lack

of badges. With a new Corvette on the horizon, production dropped to 22,940 units. The top 327-cubic-inch engine made 390 hp, while the top 427 reached 435 hp, but the big news was the incredible L88. A racing engine in disguise, this 427-cubic-inch brute had many special features, including aluminum cylinder heads that allowed it to develop 500-plus hp. With only 20 built, it's one of the rarest—and most coveted—Corvettes of all time.

Today, the 1963–67 Corvettes are nicknamed the "midyear" Corvettes, because of their production cycle in the mid-1960s. Each of the models is a classic—a true masterpiece of the automotive stylist's art.

45

Opposite: The most famous Corvette model of all time: the 1963 split-window coupe, a one-year-only body style that is now highly prized by collectors and enthusiasts worldwide. Plastic steering wheels were standard (above); the optional wood wheel was ordered by only 130 buyers in '63.
Left: Emblem detail from the fuel-injected engine of a 1963 Vette.

Pages 46–47: The ultimate Corvette: the Grand Sport. With more than 500 horsepower, these fearsome Corvette racers crushed the competition (including the very fast Shelby Cobra) in the SCCA, and were duly outlawed. Only six were built.

The speedometer on the
1964 coupe (right), sporting
a 160 mph (257kph) mark, was
slightly optimistic. Another
Corvette great: the 1967 427
big-block (below).

Opposite: The logo-embellished
gas cap that long punctuated the
rear end of the Corvette gained
new prominence on the sleek
rear-end of the classic Sting Ray.

Pages 50–51: "Aggressively elegant"
best describes the overall 1963–67
Sting Ray styling. This '63 coupe,
finished in Sebring Silver,
displays the rare knock-off
aluminum wheels.

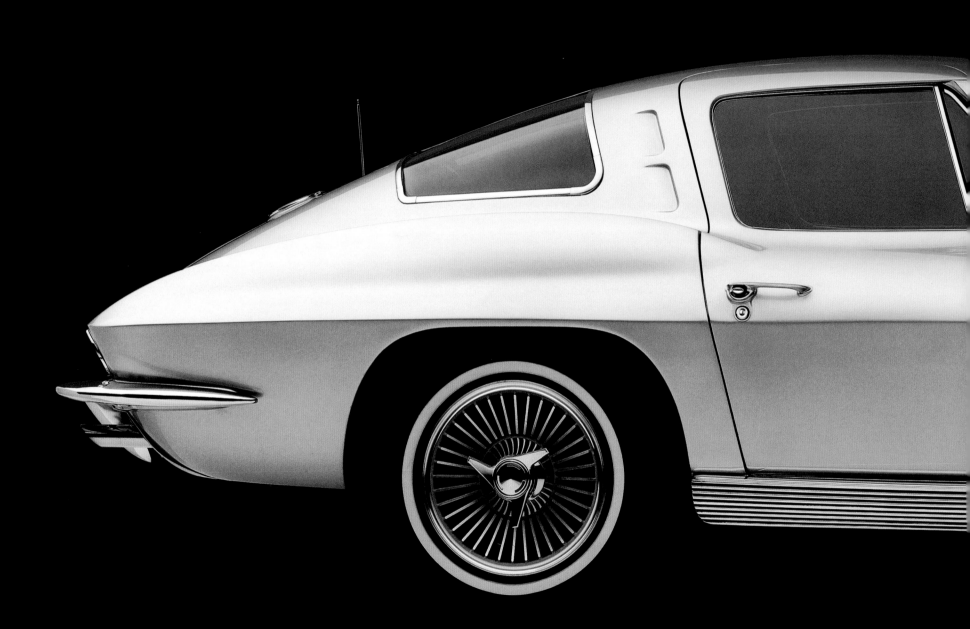

Chapter Six

1968-1972
Shark Sensations

Inspired by the Mako Shark show car, the 1968 Corvette sported an all-new streamlined body that, for its time, was revolutionary beyond comprehension. It was a bold statement of aggression, with the performance capacity to back up its hot-rod assertion.

Although the 1968 model was known simply as a Corvette, Chevrolet brought back the Stingray nameplate, now changed to a single word, the following year. With styling that mimicked the features of a shark—such as side gills in the front fender and a pointed nose with the open-mouth grille below—this era of Corvette design, which lasted until 1982, is known as the "Shark" years.

Mechanically all remained the same as in the 1967 midyear model, including the chassis, suspension, brakes, and engine options. Two body styles were offered, a convertible and a T-top coupe, with removable roof panels and rear window. The only problem that has dogged the '68 Corvette throughout its life is its poor construction. Many first-year body designs suffer because of glitches in the new tooling and unfamiliar assembly techniques, but none as much as the '68 Corvette. Nevertheless, it was popular enough to find a home in 28,566 garages.

Refinement was the key for the 1969 model. From the body shell to the reshaped interior door panels, it was a better car all around, especially in the

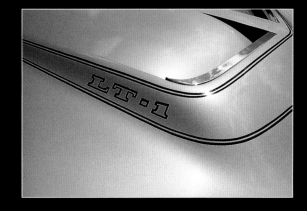

The 1972 Stingray (opposite) was the last Corvette built with chrome bumpers front and rear. The LT-1 designation (above) indicated that a solid-lifter hi-po 350-cubic-inch small-block resided under the hood.

power department. The coveted L88 option was now in its last year, and if that wasn't enough horsepower to quench your thirst for speed, there was an all-aluminum 427 engine option called the ZL1. Its tire-shredding torque and near-600 horsepower, not to mention its excessive $4,718 cost, meant that only two were ever built, thus making this the rarest Corvette ever. On a more practical note, there was the new 350-cubic-inch engine with either 300 or 350 hp and the standard 427s that had 390, 400, 430, or 435 horsepower. With 38,762 built, the '69s remain some of the most popular Corvettes.

The 1970 Corvette was the last to feature engines with high compression, but the first with the 454-cubic-inch V8 and the first to receive the LT-1 nomenclature. With the 454 LS5 putting out 390 hp, the 350-cubic-inch small-block was offered in three states of tune: 300 hp, 350 hp, and the solid lifter LT-1's 370 hp. The Stingray body shape, including the 1971–72 models, was further refined with slight fender flares, updated turn signals, and square exhaust tips. Production dropped to 17,316.

With the advent of lower compression ratios in 1971 in preparation for the catalytic converters that were soon to come, power output was reduced. The base 350 made only 270 hp, while the LT-1 was reduced to 330 hp. Meanwhile, big-block buyers could now choose from two 454s, the 365-hp LS5 or the

425-hp LS6. By the end of the year, there were a respectable 21,801 of the 1971s made.

The 1972 model was the last Stingray with front and rear chrome bumpers, an egg-crate grille, and a removable rear window. Power was quoted in net ratings, which meant even lower horsepower figures. Only the 220-hp 350 or the 255-hp LT-1 350 could be had. The sole 454 LS5 was now rated at 270 hp.

With such a wide variety of engine offerings and its distinctively attractive styling, it's no wonder these Corvettes remain the most sought after of the entire Stingray line.

The 1968 models were simply called Corvettes, but in 1969 the name Stingray returned, only this time as a single word (above). These third-generation Corvettes exhibited many unique features, such as finely designed push-in exterior door handles with separate locks (left). The exterior design (opposite) of the early Stingrays was shapely, bold, and highly distinctive. The two pairs of round rear lights continue the Corvette styling theme, used since 1961.

Another road terror, the 1971 LS5 big-block convertible boasts a 365-hp 454-cubic-inch V8 (right, top). A special hood, used only on big-block cars, vented the excess heat produced by the bigger engine. The only third-generation Corvette that wasn't called a Stingray was the 1968 model (right, bottom). Script lettering (far right) expressed the Stingray's fast-while-sitting-still styling.

1973–1977
Golden Slumber

C hevrolet, and the entire domestic automotive industry, seemed to have lost their way during the fuel-starved mid-seventies because of many new governmental regulations that strangled their engineering and styling creativity. With all the newly imposed mandates such as the Environmental Protection Agency's catalytic converters and the increasing demand by the Department of Transportation (DOT) for added crash protection, this was one era of car design when form really did follow function.

To meet the DOT's 5-mile-per-hour (8kph) regulation, a body-colored urethane front bumper, engineered to absorb impacts better than the old chrome ones, appeared on the 1973 Corvette. The rear chrome bumper remained, however, giving this Stingray a look that combined the old and the novel. The old hidden wiper system, which had malfunctioned regularly, was reworked, resulting in a restyled hood that contributed to the car's slight makeover. Added sound deadening made it quieter at high speeds while the new alloy wheel option increased its appeal. Power was reduced again, with the base 350 rated at only 190 hp; the high-horse 350 made 250 hp and the big-block 454 LS4 developed 275 hp. A total of 30,464 were built.

Not much changed for 1974 except for the use of body-colored urethane bumpers on both the front and

The 1974 Stingray (opposite) was the last of the big-block Corvettes and the last Vette offered with a dual-exhaust system without a catalytic converter.
Above: The Stingray script from a 1973 model.

the rear. But, more importantly, this was the last big-block Corvette ever built, its 454 LS4 now a mere shadow of its former self with a rating of only 270 hp. This was also the last time a true dual-exhaust system was offered without catalytic converters. The 350-hp 350 remained the same while the base V8 got an extra 5 hp. Production rose once more, to 37,502.

Although the 1975 Corvette was identical to the 1974 car (as were the 1976–77 models), the main claim to fame of the '75 was that it was the last of the convertibles. Eliminated because of safety concerns, the ragtop didn't return until 1986. Then there was the addition of catalytic converters, dropping horsepower to a measly 165 on the base engine. The only other engine option was the 205-hp version. For the performance enthusiast, the road ahead appeared rather bumpy, yet 38,465 buyers thought otherwise.

Minor upgrades were made in 1976, including a one-year-only hood. Chevrolet exploited the Vega parts bin by employing its steering wheel, much to enthusiasts' disdain. An underbelly steel pan was installed to combat the infiltration of engine heat, which was increased to help reduce emissions. With a marginal boost in horsepower to 180 and 210, demand for Corvettes rose, and 46,558 cars were ordered.

In 1977, the Stingray got its own designated steering wheel once again, fitted to a new steering column that created an additional 2 inches (5cm) of reach, making entry into the cabin easier. A redesigned console afforded more space for radio upgrades while leather upholstery became standard. Though the engines remained the same, a total of 49,213 buyers liked the improvements.

The 1973–77 models didn't offer earth-shattering performance or innovations, but they remained a good value for the money. Today that still holds true, providing buyers all the matchless allure of a Corvette Stingray for the price of a good used Cavalier.

Right: The 1973 Corvette Roadster featured new impact-absorbing bumpers painted to match the body color, and a restyled hood. (Pages 62–63): In 1975, the Corvette convertible took a bow. New Vette drivers wouldn't feel the wind in their hair for more than ten years.

Chapter Eight

1978-1982
Fastback Flyers

With two revisions already made to its original Stingray body style, the third version of the third-generation Corvette evolved into what many consider to be one of the finest shapes to ever clothe a Corvette chassis. Essentially a carbon copy of the 1968–77 models beneath its skin, the revised 1978 model sported a redesigned, racy-looking fastback rear with a large expanse of glass similar to that of the 1963–67 Sting Ray coupes, as well as a new instrument cluster that was far easier to read than the previous layout.

A total of 46,776 cars were made, but more importantly, 1978 was a year filled with special festivities at Chevrolet: the Corvette celebrated its twenty-fifth birthday and was chosen as that year's Pace Car for the Indianapolis 500. To mark these very special occasions, Chevrolet introduced two distinctive models: a two-tone silver Twenty-Fifth Anniversary Edition and a black and silver Pace Car replica. With their distinct front and rear bolt-on spoilers, both models are striking in their appearance and highly prized among Corvette collectors.

Each successive year of these later Stingray models featured special improvements. In 1979, the Pace Car's highly effective spoilers, which were said to reduce aerodynamic drag by 15 percent, were offered as an option, and halogen headlights replaced the old

Opposite: The 1980 Corvettes were sleek and light, but engine options not all that promising for Vette enthusiastes. Above: Side panel detail from a 1981 Greenwood Daytona Corvette.

sealed beam units to improve night vision. This was the most prolific year for the Vette, with an impressive 53,807 cars built.

The 1980–82 models, with their redesigned nosepieces, were lighter still because of their thinner body panels, aluminum chassis components, and stainless steel tubular exhaust headers. The 1981 Corvette has the distinction of being the last exponent of much of the old-world technology that had caused Corvette quality to slip compared to the ever-increasing competition from Europe. It was the last Corvette assembled in the old St. Louis factory, the last Corvette painted with lacquer, and the last Corvette to use a carburetor. A total of 40,606 '81s were produced, nearly equal to the previous year's 40,614.

Chevrolet opened a new assembly plant in Bowling Green, Kentucky, where they introduced Cross-Fire fuel injection on the 1982 models, the last of the aging Stingrays, which only came with automatic transmissions. With a new model soon to be released, production dropped to 25,407 cars.

Performance was nothing to write home about. Apart from the lowly 180-hp 305-cubic-inch V8 that was offered only in the 1980 model—specifically for the California market because of its increasing emissions restrictions—the 350-inch small-block was available in many different stages of tune. The

175- and 185-hp 350s of 1978 were the least desirable, especially when the 220-hp L82 version could be had. In 1979 the L82's power was increased to 225 hp, while the base engine was increased to 195 hp. The base V8 dropped to 190 hp in 1980 while the L82 version was upped to 230 hp. In 1981 only a 190-hp engine was available, which was then increased to 200 hp in 1982.

Thanks to its special combination of black and silver paint, the 1978 Pace Car had a very sinister appearance. This was also the first year of the fastback body, which provided a very aerodynamic profile. Many of the 6,502 Pace Car replicas built in 1978 were delivered without the Indianapolis 500 decals.

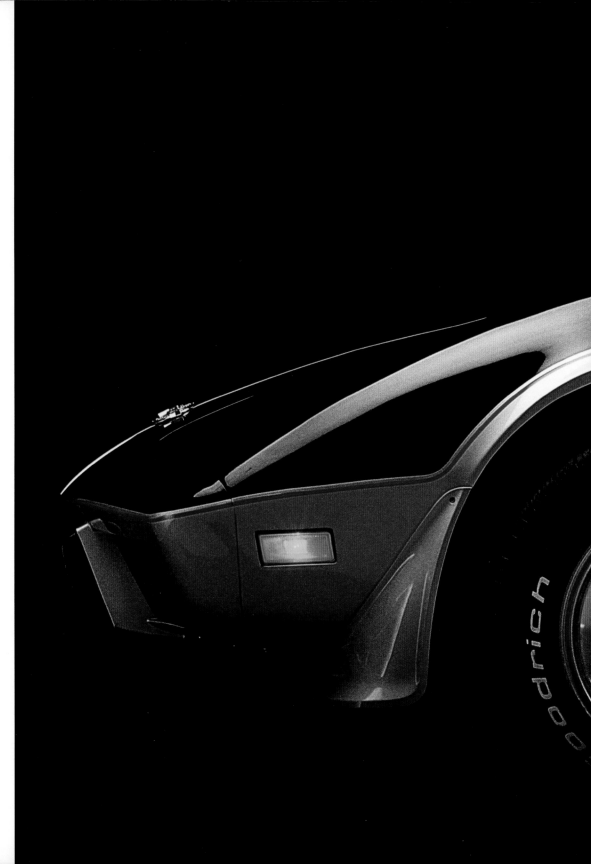

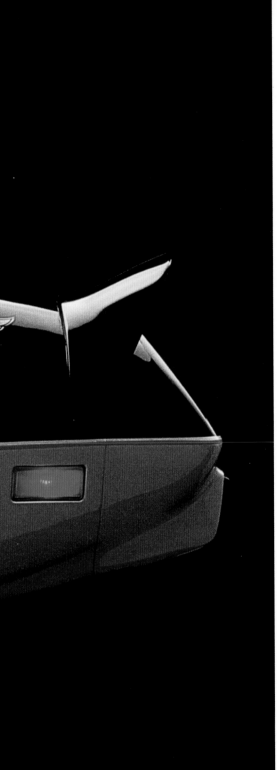

Fastback Stingrays such as this
modified '78 example (above) were
extensively used by customizers
everywhere due to their shapely
bodywork, which easily accepted
their uniquely crafted, and
sometimes odd, ideas.

Chapter Nine

1984–1990
The Electronic Age

With no Corvette available for the 1983 model year thanks to a variety of production delays and odd marketing strategies, Chevrolet brought the Corvette into the modern world in March 1983 with the all-new 1984 model. This marked the start of the fourth-generation series, a model run that lasted through the next thirteen years.

For the first time since the introduction of the 1963 Corvette, a model was designed from a clean sheet of paper, embodying nothing of previous models apart from the 1982 engine. Under the smooth contours of its contemporary shape was a specially designed chassis engineered for maximum cornering performance. The only downside was the car's harsh ride, which attracted heavy criticism from the media. Inside, drivers were greeted with a Star Wars–type display of digital instrumentation readings and a high door sill that made ingress and egress a little difficult. The power train consisted of only one engine, a 205-hp 350-cubic-inch small-block with Cross-Fire fuel injection. The public, who loved this new Corvette, snapped up 51,547 examples.

All the talk of the new Corvette's stiff ride and excessive squeaks pushed sales down to 39,729 for 1985. Unfairly inheriting the 1984 model's reputation, the 1985 Vette featured softer springs and shocks, which gave it a significantly smoother ride. It also had 25 more horsepower resulting from its new Bosch

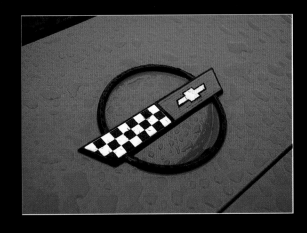

Opposite: The fourth-generation Corvettes featured contemporary styling and world-class handling ability, while electronic fuel injection made them very reliable.
Above: By the mid-1980s, even the Corvette's racing flags emblem had been reinterpreted.

electronic tuned-port fuel injection system, which also provided better performance and reliability.

Further improvements were made for 1986, including antilock brakes as standard equipment and an aluminum cylinder head option that pushed power up to 235 hp. Most importantly, 1986 witnessed the return of the convertible, with 7,315 cars so equipped out of 35,109 built. And a special Pace Car model commemorating its pacing of that year's Indy 500 was offered in yellow.

The 1987 Corvette remained unchanged apart from a few tweaks, such as roller valve lifters for a 5-hp increase and a special Z52 Sport Handling Package that combined the best components of the stiffer Z51 suspension with those of the softer base system. The big news was the availability of a pricey $19,995 twin-turbo option from Callaway Engineering, boosting power to a bold 345 hp. Of the 30,632 cars built, 184 were twin-turbos.

Better brakes were introduced in 1988 that featured dual-piston front calipers and revised rear emergency brakes. The interior was also improved, with better flow-through ventilation and carpeted sills. A special 3.07:1 axle ratio came with 245 hp; all others got the standard 240-hp version. Production totaled 22,789.

In 1989, a German-made ZF six-speed was a no-cost option that replaced the outdated four-speed. The

Z51 performance suspension was now only available with the six-speed, but a new FX3 option allowed drivers to select from three different suspension settings via a switch on the console regardless of which transmission they chose. The exterior styling and horsepower remained the same on all 26,412 cars built.

A faster, more powerful Corvette model called the ZR-1 was introduced in 1990. Based on a 350-cubic-inch small-block, the LT5 engine featured Lotus-designed aluminum block and cylinder heads with four overhead cams and thirty-two valves that developed 375 hp. With the special wide bodywork came high price tags of $58,995 for the coupe and $64,280 for the convertible. ZR-1 production in 1990 was the highest of its six-year life span, with 3,049 made, but standard Corvette production dropped to 20,597. Noteworthy changes were a revised dashboard and a new camshaft, higher compression, and a speed density intake control system that pushed horsepower on the L98 engine up to 245 and 250, depending on the axle ratio.

John Greenwood extended his noted Corvette modifications to the fourth-generation models, as evidenced by this radical-looking 1987 black convertible (right), complete with spoilers, rocker moldings, and modular wheels.

"King of the Hill" was the title given to the powerful ZR-1 Corvette. Introduced in 1990, it featured a 350-cubic-inch small-block with special aluminum twin-cam, 32-valve cylinder heads. Early versions were rated at 375 hp; later ZR-1s had 405 hp.

This is the view most familiar to all who encounter a Greenwood-built fourth-generation Corvette on the road (above). Rear light shades (opposite) were a popular modification back in the eighties.

Chapter Ten

1991–1996
The LT1 Years

Influenced by the ZR-1's wider body and squared-off taillights, the Corvette incorporated these changes for the 1991 model year. Although the standard Corvette and the ZR-1 looked alike, the ZR-1 was actually wider in the rear to help house its huge 315/35ZR 17-inch (43cm) tires. Horsepower remained the same for both models: 245 and 250 for the standard and 375 for the ZR-1. The most notable new feature was the optional Z07 adjustable suspension, perfectly suited for those who desired a firmer setting during their driver's school or auto-crossing exploits. Production of the ZR-1 dropped to 2,044 against the standard model's 18,595.

Chevrolet provided the restyled Corvette with a new 350-cubic-inch small-block engine called the LT1 in 1992. This gem was smoother, quieter, and far more reliable than any previous small-block. Some of its distinctive features included a distributorless ignition called Opti-Spark, reverse-flow cooling that cooled the free-flowing alloy cylinder heads first instead of the block, and dual oxygen sensors to optimize ignition timing. Rated at 300 hp, it instilled the fourth-generation Corvette with renewed greatness. While demand for the unchanged ZR-1 plummeted to only 502 cars, production rose slightly to 19,977 for the LT1 model. Traction control was standard in both cars.

Corvette celebrated its fortieth birthday in 1993 with a special Fortieth Anniversary Edition, whose

The last year of the fourth-generation Corvette, 1996, saw two special-edition models, a Grand Sport and the Collector's Edition (opposite) complete with ZR-1 wheels and Sebring Silver paint with special trim. Above: The sleek air intakes of a Calloway-tuned Corvette.

Ruby Red exterior and interior were exclusive to the 6,749 cars built. The LT1's horsepower rating remained at 300, while the ZR-1's LT5 engine was boosted to 405 hp. Apart from a passive keyless entry system, all else remained essentially the same. Production crept up to 21,590, 448 of which were ZR-1s.

Further refinements were made to the LT1 engine in 1994, most importantly the introduction of sequential fuel injection; power remained the same at 300 hp. Passenger-side air bags accompanied a new two-spoke steering wheel and instrumentation that glowed orange in the dark, making the interior more inviting. The ZR-1 remained the same—and so did its production total of 448. LT1 production rose to 22,882.

With an all-new Corvette just two years away, Chevrolet kept changes to the 1995 model to an absolute minimum. Visually, the most apparent change was the redesign of the air vents on the lower front fenders. And once again Corvette was picked as the Pace Car for the Indy 500, its third appearance. As before, a special Pace Car replica was produced, this time in a most unique color combination of white and dark purple with splashy graphics. Only 527 replicas were made. The year also marked the end of the ZR-1, whose production remained at 448 cars for the third year in a row, bringing total ZR-1 output to 6,939. Popular interest in the LT1 model began to drop as well—it attracted only 20,294 buyers in 1995.

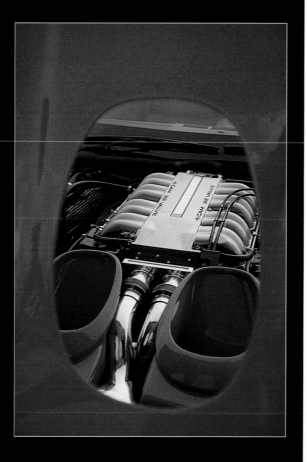

Entering its last year of production, and with the return of the Z51 suspension, the fourth-generation Corvette celebrated its long, successful run with a special Grand Sport edition. With its unique Admiral Blue paint, white stripe, and twin red hash marks on the driver's side front fender and rear fender flares, the Grand Sport looked positively racy, especially with its sinister-looking black wheels. A special one-year-only engine was included in the package. Called the LT4, this small-block V8 was an upgraded version of the LT1 that featured better flowing cylinder heads, roller rocker arms, higher compression, and a stiffer block. The result was 30 more horsepower over the LT1's already respectable 300. A second special was offered as well, called the Collector's Edition. Awash in stunning Sebring Silver paint, 5,412 were built, compared to the Grand Sport's total of 1,000. Production of the standard Corvette was only 10,755.

This powerful twin-turbo engine built by Callaway Engineering (above) pushed Corvette ownership into a class by itself. One of 2,044 ZR-1s built in 1991, this white beauty (left) features eleven-inch (28cm) -wide rear wheels housed beneath bodywork four inches (9.16cm) broader than that of standard models.

Pages 82–83: A real eye-catcher, the Callaway Super Speedster featured special aerodynamic bodywork to reduce drag, five-spoke lightweight wheels, one-piece rear light lenses, and the twin-turbo engine.

The third Corvette selected to pace the Indianapolis 500 was this 1995 convertible (opposite). With its two-tone Dark Purple and White colors, it wasn't very popular; only 527 were built.

All 1984–96 Corvettes featured a very colorful Star Wars–like digital instrumentation display (above), created by GM's Delco electronics division. Built-in vanes on the one-piece alloy wheels direct heat away from the brakes for more effective stopping performance (right).

Chromed wheels are a very
popular addition on late-model
fourth-generation Corvettes,
instilling their somewhat
conservative styling with a little
dose of pizzazz. The front air dam,
side skirts, and rear spoiler add to
the body racer look.

1997-1999
World-Class Performer

To compete against the Acura NSX, the Dodge Viper, and the Porsche 911, Chevrolet pulled out all the stops when they premiered the newest iteration of the Corvette, the C5, in January 1997. Beneath its new badge lay an all-new level of Corvette, completely unlike its predecessors. With its unique steel perimeter chassis, flexible sheet-molded compound body skin, and front-engine rear-wheel-drive layout with the transmission located in the rear for equal weight distribution, the C5 rode, handled, and cornered like no Corvette before.

The 350-cubic-inch engine was also new. The LS1 small-block is constructed entirely out of aluminum and features such notable design elements as a deep-skirted engine block that extends past the crankshaft centerline for improved stiffness, a cylinder head with identical straight-through passages for superior performance and enhanced efficiency, and a better four-bolt cylinder head pattern to help eliminate distortion and allow better sealing. All of these changes helped create an engine with reduced friction that revs easier, is far more durable, and has a higher fuel efficiency than both the LT4 and LT1 V8s. And with 345 hp and 350 pounds-feet of torque on tap, it provides a big-block-like punch.

Other goodies include an electronic drive-by-wire throttle, a distributorless ignition with individual coil packs for each spark plug, run-flat Goodyear perfor-

The one Corvette not to be seen in if you don't like people staring at you, the 1998 Pace Car (opposite)—with its wild purple and yellow color scheme—is a real magnet for attention.
Above: For those looking for something more subtle, the hot 1998 Vette also came in a classy pewter gray metallic.

mance tires on 17-inch (43cm) front and 18-inch (46cm) rear wheels, and, as odd as it may seem, a floor that consists of a thin layer of balsa wood—for its excellent sound absorption qualities—sandwiched between two layers of sheet metal to help reduce the infiltration of noise into the cabin. It's simple, yes, but very effective.

In the power train department, only the one LS1 engine is available. The two transmission choices consist of the 4L60-E four-speed automatic or the T-56 six-speed gearbox. Other options include four-wheel disc brakes with antilock brakes, traction control, and active handling to prevent the car from spinning out.

The body configurations come in three different styles: a coupe with a removable roof panel in 1997; a convertible, introduced in 1998; and the new lightweight 1999 hardtop, which can be had only with the six-speed gearbox and stiffer Z51 performance suspension. Regardless of which model you choose, the C5 Corvette is one of the greatest sports cars ever built.

In keeping with tradition, a 1998 Pace Car replica was produced to celebrate the Corvette's fourth appearance at the Indianapolis 500. Built in convertible form only, this is the most radical-looking production Corvette ever made, with its purple exterior complemented by a dazzling bright yellow interior and wheels, and bold graphics flowing over the rear fender. It's a real head-turner that only 1,158 owners will get to enjoy.

The C5 sums up everything that's good about today's car designs, with its solidity of construction, user-friendly interior, true aerodynamic styling, almost maintenance-free durability, and low environmentally harmful emissions. It's a contemporary Corvette for contemporary expectations, and it's come a long way from the little white roadster that introduced European-styled sports car fun to the United States.

Introduced in 1998, the C5 convertible (left) is the best driving convertible ever: solid, stiff, and free of squeaks and rattles—a pure pleasure machine. The C5's instrumentation (above) is analog. A black light illuminates the white numbers, eliminating strain on the driver's eyes. Pages 92–93: The styling of the 1997 C5 coupe is a blend of several different cars, including the Acura NSX, Pontiac Firebird, Ferrari 456 GT, and Mazda RX7. But the overall appearance is pure Corvette.

Corvette Engine Options

YEAR	CUBIC INCH	STANDARD HORSEPOWER	OPTIONAL HORSEPOWER	YEAR	CUBIC INCH	STANDARD HORSEPOWER	OPTIONAL HORSEPOWER
1953	235.5	150	—	1976–7	350	180	210
1954	235.5	150	155	1978	350	185	220
1955	235.5	150	155	1979	350	195	225
	265	210	—	1980	350	190	230
1956	265	210	225, 240	1980	305	180	—
1957	283	220	245, 250, 270, 283	1981	350	190	—
1958–9	283	230	245, 250, 270, 290	1982	350	200	—
1960	283	230	245, 270, 275, 315	1984	350	205	—
1961	283	230	245, 275, 315	1985	350	230	—
1962–3	327	250	300, 340, 370	1986	350	230	—
1964	327	250	300, 364, 375	1987	350	240	—
1965	327	250	300, 350, 365, 375	1988	350	240	245
	396	425	—	1989	350	240	245
1966	327	250	350	1990	350	240	250
	427	390	425, 450		350/ ZR-1	375	—
1967	327	300	350	1991	350	245	—
	427	390	400, 430, 435		350/ ZR-1	375	—
1968	327	300	350	1992	350	300	—
	427	390	400, 435		350/ ZR-1	405	—
1969	350	300	350	1993	350	300	—
	427	390	400, 435		350/ ZR-1	405	—
1970	350	300	350, 370	1994	350	300	—
	454	390	—		350/ ZR-1	405	—
1971	350	270	330	1995	350	300	—
	454	365	425		350/ ZR-1	405	—
1972	350	200	255	1996	350	300	330
	454	270	—	1997	350	345	—
1973	350	190	250	1998	350	345	—
	454	275	—	1999	350	345	—
1974	350	195	250				
1974	454	270	—				
1975	350	165	205				

Index

Photo Credits

©George Kamper: pp. 2, 16–17, 24–25, 26–27, 31, 35, 44, 50–51, 54 right, 54–55, 80–81. ©Ron Kimball: pp. 5, 10, 12–13, 18, 20–21, 22–23, 30 bottom left, 32–33, 34 left, 35, 36, 38, 40–41, 41 top right, 42, 46–47, 48 left, 58, 66–68, 69, 70, 72–73, 74–75, 76, 77, 78, 82–83, 84, 86–87, 88, 89, 90–91, 92–93. ©Mike Mueller: pp. 15, 19, 25 right, 26 left, 28, 30 bottom right, 34 right, 41 bottom right, 48 right, 49, 52, 53, 56 top left, 56 bottom left, 91 right. ©D. Randy Riggs: pp. 6–7, 8, 9, 11, 14–15, 21 right, 29, 38 bottom, 43, 45 left, 45 right, 54 left, 56–57, 71, 79, 81 right, 85 left. ©Richard Lentinello: pp. 37, 39. Automobile Quarterly: pp. 30 top, 59, 60–61, 62–63, 64, 65. Zone Five Photo/©Robert Genat: 85 right.